William R. Hearst and Controversy

By Rich Linville

ISBN: 9798709800236

You might say that I was born with a silver spoon in my mouth. You should be so lucky. My name is William Randolph Hearst.

I was the only son of George Hearst, a wealthy gold, silver and copper mine owner and United States senator of California from 1886 to 1891.

After attending Harvard College for two years, I was expelled for my antics like sponsoring massive beer parties in Harvard Square and sending chamber pots to my professors with their images depicted within the bowls. Some people can't take a rich man's jokes!

In 1880, my father acquired the San Francisco Examiner newspaper. He primarily used the Examiner to promote the Democratic Party and to praise the party's actions, especially when they were under public attack.

In 1887, at the age of 23, I insisted on taking control of the struggling San Francisco Examiner newspaper. I remade the newspaper into a blend of reformist investigative reporting and lurid sensationalism, and within two years it was showing a profit. Controversy makes me lots of money!

In 1895, I purchased an unsuccessful New York newspaper. I hired exceptional writers and from a rival publisher I stole writers such as Richard F. Outcault, who drew the Yellow Kid cartoons. I used many drawings and headlines that slapped you in the face with sensational articles on crime and false-scientific topics. I was eager to go to war in foreign affairs.

Competition can sometimes be good or it can be bad. I became involved in a series of newspaper circulation wars. My newspaper used sensationalistic reporting and promotional schemes.
I reduced its price to one cent. Competition between two papers, included rival Yellow Kid cartoons, soon gave rise to the term yellow journalism, meaning the "Fake News" of the 1800's.

I became a war hawk after a rebellion broke out in Cuba in 1895. Competing with another newspaper for headlines, we were called "yellow press" because we often covered the revolution inaccurately. Newspaper publishers Joseph Pulitzer and I were each dressed as the Yellow Kid comics character in a political cartoon. We were each claiming to have caused the Spanish-American War. War sells newspapers. I make money!

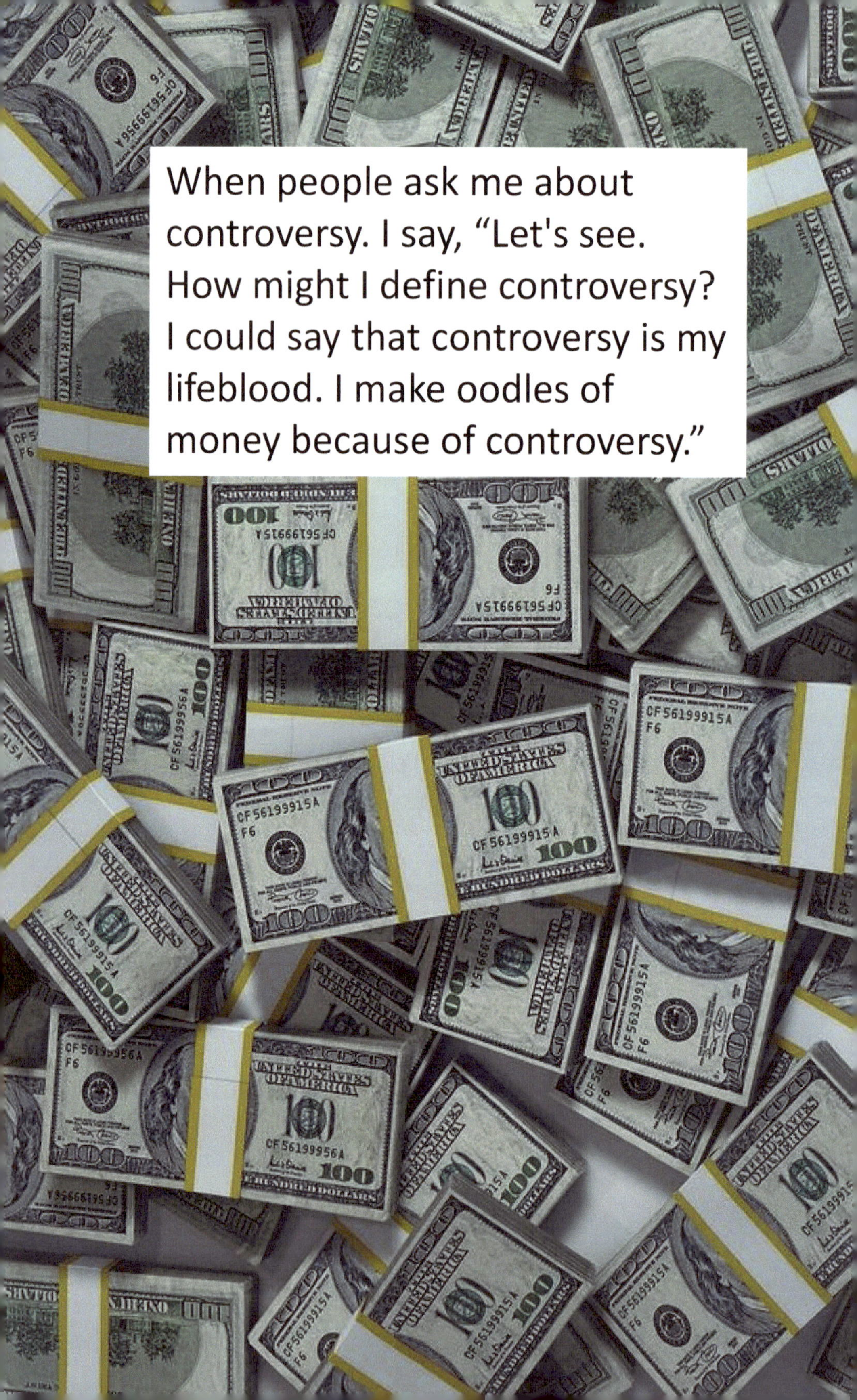
When people ask me about controversy. I say, "Let's see. How might I define controversy? I could say that controversy is my lifeblood. I make oodles of money because of controversy."

I am an American newspaper publisher who has built up the nation's largest newspaper chain in what I like to call, "The Hearst Publishing Empire". My methods profoundly influence American journalism. I also encourage companies like automobile manufacturers and soda companies to pay me to advertise in my newspapers.

While in the U.S. House of Representatives from 1903 to 1907, I received considerable support for the Democratic presidential nomination in 1904. I came within 3,000 votes of winning the 1905 election for mayor of New York City. In 1906, I lost to Charles Evans Hughes in the election for governor of New York.

In 1909, I suffered a defeat running for election as New York City mayor. Rejected in my political ambitions, I still complained about the British Empire. I was opposed to U.S. entry into World War I and criticized the League of Nations and the World Court. Isolationism was my viewpoint for American.

In the 1920's, I built a
grand castle on a 240,000 acre
(97,000 hectare) ranch in San
Simeon, California.

I furnished this residential complex with a large collection of expensive antiques and art objects that I had bought in Europe.

During the 1920's, I became a strong Democrat. I warned everyone against the dangers of big government, of unchecked federal power that could infringe on the individual rights of all Americans.

I also published books of fiction and produced motion pictures featuring the actress Marion Davies.

By 1925, I had started or acquired newspapers in every part of the United States, as well as some magazines.

At the peak of my fortune, in 1935, I owned 28 major newspapers and 18 magazines, along with many radio stations, movie companies, and news services. I finally was the owner of my own Hearst Publishing Empire.

But my own personal extravagances and the Great Depression of the 1930's soon seriously weakened my finances. I had to sell my faltering newspapers or consolidate them. In 1937 I was forced to sell off some of my art collection.

By 1940, I had lost personal control of my publishing empire that I had built. I lived the last years of his life alone with no friends. My life was the basis for the movie *Citizen Kane* (1941).

After I supported FDR in 1932, I soon became highly critical of the New Deal. My newspapers supported big business instead of organized labor. I condemned higher income tax laws as a persecution of the "successful."

I broke with FDR in 1935 and supported the Republican Alf Landon who lost. I was losing my power as an influencer of American politics.

Without allowing rebuttals, my newspapers ran columns by Nazi leader Hermann Göring and Hitler himself, as well as Mussolini and other dictators in Europe and Latin America. Many Americans were upset about those newspaper columns.

Because medical care was not available in my remote location, I left my San Simeon estate in 1947 to seek medical care. I died in Beverly Hills on August 14, 1951, at the age of 88. I was interred in the Hearst family mausoleum at the Cypress Lawn Cemetery in Colma, California, which my parents had established. Do I have any regrets about my life and my choices? I died with no friends, hated by many. What do you think?

Dedicated to my lovely wife Sulastri and my grandchildren Mia and Kai as well as everyone who wants to learn history.

For over 40 years, I have enjoyed teaching at elementary, high school and college levels.

Please review after reading. Your review makes a difference. Also, please visit my author page and follow to get new releases: Amazon.com/author/richlinville

Illustrations from PixaBay, Wiki, and purchased from Edu-Clips.com.

Please check out my books at bookstores and online under the name Rich Linville.

Cold War

1945 to 1991

By Rich Linville

Wolves

by Rich Linville

My Alaskan Race
by Huskie Dog
From my point of view
Written by Rich Linville

My Basketball Blues

from the Basketball's Point of View

Written by Rich Linville

My Rocky Adventure!
By Rocky Magma
Written by Rich Linville

Someday I'd like to be
a rock instead of magma

Sharks

by Rich Linville

9 798709 800236